# Hidden

M000198482

## A Tribute to Unspoken Heroes

Author
**Marcus Rain Pena**

**Scan QR code below
to shop or follow my
social media pages**

# NOTES

# Dedication

I want to dedicate this book to someone who doesn't give up no matter what the obstacle is. To someone who is not only an amazing person, kindhearted soul but also an outstanding soldier. Someone who I am blessed to call my nephew, Colton Lyvers.

He is the example of determination, hard work and always striving for success. No matter what twists and turns life has thrown at him he never seems to miss a beat. If life throws you lemons, he knows how to make lemonade. So, pour me another round.

Thank you for all that you have done and thank you for the service to our country. You are an unspoken hero.

# Acknowledgement

I would like to acknowledge all the people that supported and believed in me. Always pushed me to never give up. To family, friends, followers and fans that have come to realize it is not just poetry, but it is finding the inner subconscious emotions that we hold in and lock away. I would like to thank all the unspoken heroes, the ones that don't get acknowledged or appreciated on an everyday basis. The ones that wear capes underneath their uniforms. These are just a few of many heroes: teachers, police officers, firefighters, nurses, doctors, paramedics, moms, dads, cooks, servers, maintenance employees, service pets, military, etc....

Special shout out to Cypher for his artwork.
**Follow him on IG: @cypherologist**

To Ashley Fincher, **Follow her on FB ashcreations.913**
To Ali Haider, Thank you for formatting the book.
To everyone in the pictures:
Enoc and Mariana Salazar-Ruiz, Priscilla Morin, Tyler and Troy Dotson, Anthony Gardner, SSG Howard and Family,William Graham II, Sgt Maisonet and son, SSG Rhoten Dorian, Sgt Garcia John, Sean Garcia, SSG Hans Clinton and family, Sgt Salazar, Sgt Ramirez, Anthony Gardner, Sgt Vazquez Hector, Sgt Wilson, 1st Sgt Jones Rodney, Lemon, Christian Diaz and Valentina Diaz, Marcus Pena, Alfredo Pena Jr, John Becerra, Albert Arriaga, Randy Smith, Officer I. Rodriguez with the Clovis Police Department, Simon Garcia, Sergeant First Class Michael Leongtave, Conley Family, SSG Nava Amy, Sgt Minas Justin, SSG Amos Clay, Captain Lopez Herbes, Camille, Philip Vargas A.K.A. Philly, Alante Love, SSG

Chapman, Angel Chapman thank you for your amazing service as a teacher.
In loving memory of Mrs. Evangeline "Vangie" Alaniz

Shutterstock Images: digital storm, Getmilitaryphotos, Alexander Smulskiy, PRESSLAB, BPTU, Cheryl Casey, Barilo_Picture, andrea crisante, altanaka, I_B, pimchawee, Black Salmon, Jos Temprano, Maksim Toome, Pushish Images, Photographee.eu, Volodymyr TVERDOKHLIB, REDAV, KARTESS, Irina_iris, Realstock

## Description of Book

Hidden Secrets is part 2 of a five series set that takes a dive into the subconscious feelings, thoughts and emotions of the reader. Every poem is written with the intent that an individual can relate to whether its by personal experience or knowing someone with a similar situation.

# Table of Contents

# Chapter 1
# Unspoken Heroes

# I am

I am your hero
The hero in the shadows
Protector till the end
I stand for what I believe
What I believe in is
Justice, peace and happiness
I am
A SOLDIER
A MARINE
A SAILOR
A GUARDSMAN
AN AIRMAN
I am a member of the United States Military

# Firefighter Hero

I lay my head to rest
Eyes were heavier than I thought
I slowly drifted away into the world of dreams
Feeling happy slowly faded away
I started to cough profusely; my chest is tightening up
I opened my eyes terrified at what could be happening
I was scared, lost and disoriented
This had to be a nightmare. Watching everything around
me embrace in smoke
Listening to the fire roar, like the king of the jungle
dominates its prey
I was too shocked to cry, a lifetime of memories burned in
seconds
I knew I had to leave this subjected reality of hell on earth
As I quickly dropped to the ground to make way to my
escape, I could hear voices in the background
I tried to shout and scream for help but all I could get out
was a small screech
Tears ran down my face
My heart pounding knowing the end was near
Not of this fire but of my life
Losing strength, I felt myself getting more tired, unable to
crawl out, unable to move
My body was weak, I dropped completely down and
faded away
I was back in this subconscious world, a dream or a
nightmare?
I felt my body get lifted, "are you okay, don't let go."
Unsure what was going on but feeling a sense of relief
and trust in this person

Before I could configure what was going on or where I
was, I felt a breath of fresh air
As I coughed, no more heat surrounded me
I was going to live

Firefighters the unspoken hero

# My Daddy is a Hero

Your music soft and sweet
Singing me lullabies
Bringing my screaming and cries to a hush in the night
Shielding me with protection in your arms
In a world so dark, you showed me the beauty and
delight
Told me you would be by my side the whole ride
Fighting my sleep to not miss a second of your happiness
Not a moment passes that I don't think of you
You are my hero
My daddy

## Police Officers

I didn't do it for the pay
It wasn't for recognition at the end of the day
Not a moment passes that I don't worry
What's the end of this call going to result in?
Worry and distress flood my mind
I patrol the streets searching for crime
Like a hero in a comic book
However, the ending is not always rainbows and
butterflies
Fear is not an option
A police officers job never ends

# Reality

Another day in the office as a soldier in combat
Long convoy ride down a pothole filled road
Nothing out of the ordinary
Everyone in the Humvee laughing and listening to music
I was dozing off
When out of nowhere
Shots fired in the distance
Reality kicked in, I was scared and I was lost
This can't be happening; this can't be real

# Super-Women

I am strong, hardworking, determined
I am a leader, I am powerful
Call me a friend, a sister, a mother, a doctor
A teacher, a soldier, a woman

I am many things
Nothing compares to my strength, my love and my
passion

Listen to me as I pursue my dreams and create a reality
of happiness
In a world so tough I had to show I am tougher
Proving I could handle anything because I am more than
just a sweet smile, a beautiful face and a loving heart
I am ME!
I am a woman

27

# Roll Call

I couldn't believe the news, it couldn't be true
I won't accept losing you
No, please tell me the news is wrong, please come out
from wherever your hiding
This joke is not funny anymore
I need you...I said I need you dammit
I go to work the next day
Still in denial, praying you show up
Why don't you show up?!
I'm begging you to come back as I scream it in my head
over and over again
I look at where you would usually be
Talking to all the other soldiers because everyone had to
know you
I show up to formation, but you never arrive
I lie to myself that this isn't the last formation they will say
your name
Then it begins...Roll Call
Name by name they call us out. You hear a soldier's
name called and they reply, "Here First Sergeant", the
next soldier is called and responds with, "Present First
Sergeant".
This continues until they say your name
No response, no answer, and finally for the last time
WHY!!
Why won't you answer
Tears run down my face as though they are running from
the truth too
Then I realized
I lost a friend, hero, my brother in arms

# Last Breath

I held your hand while you said goodbye
Even soldier's cry
A tear ran down my cheek
You said "Don't look at it as dying,
Look at it as I am reporting to my next duty station"
As I watched you take your last breath

## Doctors

Thank you for being there
When I needed you unexpectedly
Those random nights I couldn't sleep because everything
hurt
You didn't make me feel awkward when I was pale to the
bone and re-serving you my lunch that I couldn't hold
down

Whatever illness wants to knock me down
You never hesitate to stand up for me
Like the hero you won't admit you are
Always on call
Even at your most unavailable times
Waiting for your signal to save the day
With your secret power of knowledge and medicine

You are not just a doctor but a hero

# Nightmares

I was asked when was the last time I was in the war
I said
Every night that I close my eyes

# Nurses

Sometimes people think nurses are just the doctor's
secretary or are here to simply check your weight and
vitals
However, that is wrong, they are much more

Nurses are the warm welcoming smile that is given to you
as you enter the door
Even if they are still at work after hitting a 12-hour day
They comfort you from your worries
Answer all the absurd questions
Even when we all ask the same question a million times

They monitor your life no matter how big or small your
emergency is
Whether its fever or cardiac arrest or anything in between
They stress continuously over finding the right patient
care plan
They stand up for us as the advocate for our health and
well-being

Then they give us the assurance on how to manage our
illness
Not only educating us but breaking it down in layman's
terms because they know we are not informed on what
medical terminology is

They are not just nurses they are heroes and by the way
don't tell anyone this secret
They have capes on underneath those scrubs but
remember shhh dont tell anyone

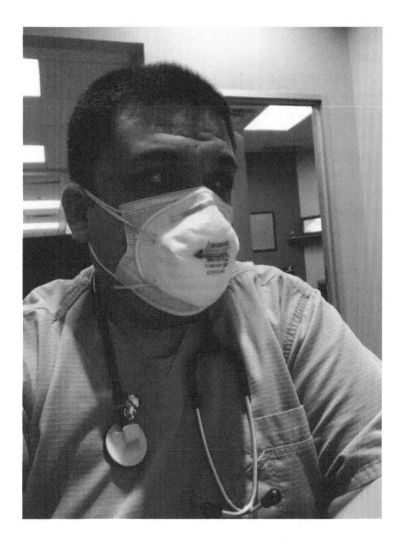

## Mental Warfare

You think because I'm a soldier
I don't feel pain
You think because I fight in a war I don't fight my own
demons
I'm tough on the outside
Little do you know
I'm broken on the inside
I'm crying, I'm dying
I'm all alone in a world full of people
They don't understand me
PTSD is a silent killer
Now watch me play pretend
Smile and carry on with the day
A day I wish would end
I'm like an actor in a movie
However, the scene won't end
Come on director say cut

## Building Blocks

Thank You Teachers...

You were there in the beginning showing me to raise my
hand and be excited for everyday
You showed me how to whisper with my inside voice
You taught me my ABC's and 123's
You explained simple math to me and told me to never
give up
Everything from reading, to writing complete sentences
you were always there

Thank You Teachers....

For showing us how to open our minds to research
papers and book reports
Not to mention projects and teamwork.
Oh, and who could forget the fun but gross dissections
Or the dreadful public speaking essays

Thank You Teachers....

You never gave up on me, even if I had to stay after class
to learn how to find X
When I couldn't even figure out my own ex.
It was an emotional roller coaster that I couldn't get off of.
Thinking my whole world would end if I wasn't the most
popular
However, you kept paving the way

Thank You Teachers...

I'm in college now and you're still guiding me
Feeling like a grown up because I must pay for my own
classes
Every day I get closer to graduating with my degree

In the end
I write my only way to express my gratitude towards you
all
My previous teachers and professors, thank you for being
the building blocks to my future

# Pet Hero

Heroes come from all parts of the world
Some are doctors, teachers, police officers, firefighters
and even military personnel
Not to mention so much more
My hero is
The protector of my happiness
A fighter for my attention
Loyal until the end
My hero brings warmth to my heart with
The endless love
My hero is my pet

# Goodnight

I stare at you through the phone
As you close your eyes
Sleep tight baby
Daddy's got to work tonight
Don't worry everything will be alright
Woken abruptly
Nightmares become reality
Gunshots in the background
Shake off the sleep
Time to fight
I'm scared but I hide my fear behind my rifle
Deep breathing
I hear screaming
Bodies dropping
Rapid fire not stopping
Everything is happening so fast
Not able to think
Eyes moving so fast, scanning around
Then without a moment's notice
I feel a piercing pain strike my body
It takes my breath away
Then I think to myself
As I close my eyes
Sleep tight baby
Daddy's got to work tonight
Don't worry everything will be alright

## Angel of Freedom

I love it when you smile and laugh so hard that your nose
makes a snorting sound.
You make the cutest faces while you daydream and twirl
your hair around your finger.
It's so adorable watching you get frustrated, then stomp
one foot down as you walk away.
The memories we shared got me through the toughest
days in the war
Bragging to my comrades about you writing me, showing
off your picture to all the other service members.
It seems like a distant memory. A smile in the clouds
Driving towards rainbows we will never find the end too
but loving the memories and laughter along the journey
Wishing I could be there to watch you read this letter.
This moment of happiness
If you're reading this, it means I'm gone but I'll always be
in your heart. That means I became an angel while
fighting in combat. Fighting for what I believed in.
Fighting for freedom, fighting for peace.

Love Always,
Your Toy Soldier

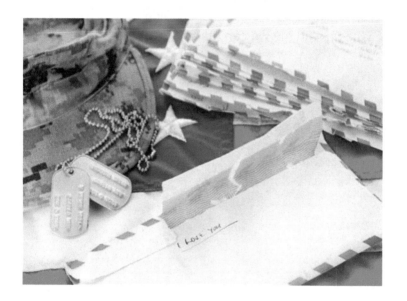

# Stand Up Please

Alexander Hamilton said if you don't stand for something,
you'll fall for anything
Today I stand up for what I believe in
I stand up for myself
Yet I stand up for everyone
Who couldn't, wouldn't and or shouldn't
Stand up with me we can make a difference

# Chapter 2
# Unmasked Sadness

# Letter to Heaven

My Love,

I don't know what to be without you around. I'm still trying to understand how you could leave me here alone. I wish you were here to hold me and make it all better like you always do. I have been so blessed to have been part of your life. You have taught me so much about myself and life and for that I am forever grateful. You have given me so many wonderful memories and so much happiness over the years that I wouldn't trade for anything. You will always have a special place in my heart. There's nothing like you and I! Our kids miss you. Our little family will never be the same.
I love you always...

## Ocean Tears

Missed you all day today, even more than usual. I keep my toes in the sand and thought about the hundreds of memories we made together. I even caught a couple waves today! The whole time I was wishing you were there. Smiling that goofy smile and laughing when I wiped out and just cheering me on when I finally caught one. You meant the world to me, I'm sorry if I didn't tell you enough but thanks for always being there for me no matter what. You were an amazing friend and made this life a better place! Sending love to you today

Love & Miss you forever and ever

# Till Tomorrow

I miss you friend; I will love you forever.
You were always so true to me; you had my back no
matter what and meant the world to me
Thanks for holding my hand when I needed a friend, and
for lending a shoulder for so many of my tears.
You changed a part of my heart forever friend. Forever till
we meet again

## It's not what

You kissed him in front of me
It was an accident you insisted
It wasn't supposed to happen
Shaking my head in confusion
Balling my fist in anger

Why...what are you doing
I was at a loss for words
Flabbergasted
Completely dumbfounded by the thought
As it replays in my head
Making me nauseous reliving the moment
Again and again

You know what, kissing him wasn't an accident
Getting caught by me was
But to me honey
The ONLY real accident was loving you

# Picture This

I go to bed looking at your picture and hope it will stop the pain
In hopes the picture will become reality
That you walk in the room and tell me you love me, and everything is good
None of this ever happens

# Monet

Who am I to judge?
You accept me for who I am
Living a life of misery and despair
Who would listen, who would care?
A beautiful painting on the wall
In the distance I see you
But can't touch you
Reaching out to grab you
To only feel air
So close but so far
I can smell your sweet perfume
The way your smile can light up a room
Staring in your eyes
Holding tight on your hips
Feeling your sweet soft lips
I open my eyes to realize you're not there
How could this be a dream

# Who's Crying Now

You lied and blamed it on me
You wanted a break blamed it on me
You cheated and blamed it on me
I found happiness while you were gone
You said, how could I find someone else
I thought you cared, I thought you loved me
I said it's ok we're done
Blame it on Me!!!

# Happy Birthday

It happens every year
It never gets any easier
It was your favorite holiday
Now it's the saddest day of the year
Happy Birthday
Another year has passed
Since you passed
I love you and miss you so much!!
I wish I could go back in time to stop you
But now I'm looking up into the night sky
Thinking about you
Maybe your looking down
Thinking about me

# Think Twice

You always told me that I was nothing but a
disappointment
Everything that you used to tell me
Now makes me think twice
Before I make a decision
Before I make a mistake
I think twice
I don't want to be where I used to be in your life
I don't want to be second anymore
I don't even want to have you around
Everything about you makes me think twice
Fuck I hate you; I can't stand you, just the thought of
looking at you makes me sick
I can't even think of you in my mind
I wouldn't want to go into a direction that makes me want
to lean towards you
You're the epitome of fucking disgust I don't even want to
think of it.
For a matter of fact, I couldn't even consider or even
imagine you
Thoughts of you hinder my happiness. The thought of
you taking care of me or looking at me in any other way
pisses me off
You know what, just fuck you and get out of my life and
get going because I never want to see you, let alone be
involved in your life
Every time I think I'm doing great it reminds me that…
I'm nothing more than a mistake

# Detox

I had to leave the relationship
Just seeing you in a photo was toxic
You pose a threat to my heart

# 9mm

Today I lay my head down to rest
Knowing I gave it my best
Exhausted at all the attempts and test
I gave you my all
To my knees I fall
Words can't explain
The unhappiness I gain
From simply hearing my damn name
A name you gave me
Supposedly picked with love
Yes, you named me after yourself
However only because you are a greedy son of a bitch
Sometimes I meet people who say I look like you and I
sound like you too
Ugh it makes me mad; a dictionary can't define my hate
for you
Now I stand in front of the mirror
Gun in hand
Locked and loaded
Tomorrow is a new beginning
Today I lay my head down to rest
Knowing I gave it my best
Exhausted at all the attempts and test

# Enkephalin

No words can ever mend my broken heart for you
What I would do to have one more day by your side
I love you to the moon and back
Rest easy and wait for me at the gates

# No More

Today I stared into a blank abyss
Wishing, hoping
I'm praying that I can fight the pain, the heartache, the trouble
But I didn't know where it came from
Today
I lost my battle to anxiety

# My Oh My

My pillow is filled with tears
My dreams show me my fears
My life feels like a lie
The animosity grew stronger between my feelings and
emotions
My heart and my happiness
My anger, my hate
The future of my fate
I'm lost, I'm confused
The pain
The abuse
Physical or emotional
It all becomes one at some point or another
I take it, I take it, but I can't give any more

# Numb

I worked out extra hard today in the gym
In hopes the pain in my body would numb the pain in my heart
In hopes the sweat coming down from my brow would hide the sweat of pain coming down my eyes

# Lost for Words

I said hello
When I should have said goodbye
I said I missed you
Even when I didn't need you
I told you I love you even when I hated you
I said I do
When deep down inside I don't
I said goodnight
When I should have said nothing at all
But when I woke to you gone and a note on your pillow, it said
I left because I couldn't fake another day of loving you

## One Sided Love

You said you love me
You would always stand by my side
We made a promise to be each other's forever
I guess promises are meant to be broken
Because forever never came
Now I walk alone
My heart crushed to the ground
Staring at my phone
No ring not even a sound
This must be what broken promises sound like

# Heart Beaten

Remembering you is easy
I do it everyday
But missing you is a heartache
That I wish would go away
Just like you did from my life

# Call of the Void

I cried myself to sleep
Stare deep into the void
Wishing on every star
Why did you have to go?
I needed you so much
You walked out that door
You went off into the war
I begged you to stay
But all you could say
Is I'm already gone
Wonder hopelessly
Throughout the day
Why does it have to be this way

# My Anchor

I used to think I was on top of the world
Until I lost you
Then I lost myself
My pity my sorrow my best friend

# wHATEver

What started as fate
Turned to
HATE
You're the cancer of my life
The thought of you is straight disgust
No love, no trust
All you ever did was scream and shout
Now you make me live in a life of mistrust and doubt
All because you hurt me
You broke me
Shattered my confidence
Belittled me to nothing
However, I'm the idiot
I loved you, exactly LOVED you
For who you are
NOT
For anything you ever did for me
I hate you

## Red Flags

I should have seen those red flags
I should have said something
I feel like I failed him
Now we must pick up the pieces and get through the loss
of you
We love you daddy

# 22

### Day 1

Depression is a wound that never heals
It acts as a virus, it eats at the person
Its symptoms affect everyone
Suffering right before your very eyes
My happiness is a disguise
The laughter and smile it's all a lie
I have my ups and downs just like everyone else
When I was deployed
I had dreams of committing suicide
Bringing this pain to an end
I even thought about it during my every day
It got to the point where I was getting comfortable with
the thought
One day I was alone in a room
I broke down in tears fighting my very own fears

### Day 22

It was that moment that I realized I needed help
I need to survive this inner battle
I dropped to my knees and begged for a sign
Then I saw an image, a daydream if you may,
Of my kids, myself, family and my parents
So, I search for help to get me through this inner trauma
When I went through it I was strong so strong but today I
am broken
Like glass with a hammer shattering my soul

# Next

You said I was a good guy, but you wanted a bad boy
A more exciting man
You left me for the bad boy you always wanted
The bad boy cheated on you for another girl
Oh, how the tables have turned

# Love Me, Please

Everything is perfect like eating a cupcake topped with
chocolate chips, while on a swing in the middle of fall

Young and in love with the sweet smell of you as you
hold me tight
Were so different but our hearts came similar to a chaotic
mess or a beautiful disaster
You're the sin to my blessing

I watched as a rock hit the window, causing a small crack
that kept growing
Our relationship was like the perfect cathedral window,
overseeing the city

Then it started
What seemed harmless you would think
Spending more time on your phone, working late, even
later at night, text messages that were from your friend.
Then I grew the courage to ask

Who is she?

## Burr

I lay in the dark, waiting for the night of bad dreams to
pass
Squeezing my eyes shut while laying in bed
Wishing that things were different, hoping things will get
better
Everything was a gloom, everything made me think twice
Now breathing heavy, trying to catch my breath
All I can think about is how much I hate anxiety,
depression
But this too shall pass

# Struggle

Living a real-life eating ramen noodles and oatmeal in bread
They don't know about walking to the laundromat with big ass bags of clothes, boiling water on the stove for baths, lighting candles in the house because the power went off but it wasn't storming.

They DON'T know about having shoes only for school, hand me downs, sleeping on the couch or floor.
They DON'T know about getting food at a food pantry, sleeping fully clothed and all the family in one room because the heat was off or turning the oven on to heat the house.
They DON'T know about hand washing clothes in the tub & drying it by the heater.
If you haven't struggled through real shit, I don't expect you to understand me or my ambition to get rid of my generational curses.
I never ate from a silver spoon so I will never make fun of another person's struggle.
I will work night and day to overcome and ensure my family never struggles the way we did when we were kids.
I came from a BIG strong family, where we learned to survive no matter what and it made me who I am today

# Chapter 3
# Undercover Thoughts

## Stolen Tomorrow

I must say
Treasure the moment like it is the last and always say
goodbye like you will never see them again

# Betrayal

You lead me on right now
To invite me in tonight
To fuck me over by tomorrow

## Delusions

Don't love me today
And
Leave me tomorrow

## Midnight Snack

I'm tired of being your midnight snack
When you crave something different that you don't have
at home

## Inner Beauty

When you open your eyes and realize
I'm not perfect, but I'm perfect just the way I am

# Through Someone Else's Eyes

Take a moment
Take a glance
Take a deep breath as you step into this trance
It would only take a few minutes
To see through someone else's eyes
To understand their pain
For it doesn't last forever
And that compassion is something more than just a
feeling
Never judge someone
Until you have seen things through their eyes
You may be surprised by the things you will see

## Common Cents

I don't take charity but
You always want to give me your two cents

# Who Me?

Am I the sinner or the sin?

# Au Revoir

I thought I would hate you
But once you left
I realized
I don't hate my past
I learn from it

# ?

Just because you don't love me doesn't mean no one will

# Gasping for Life

They say I can be strong I can overcome my anxiety and
my depression
But who are they to say?
They are not ME
They do not cry, they do not hurt, they do not scream at
nothing and feel everything
While not feeling anything at all

# Judgmental

You judge me because I'm quiet
You judge me because I'm different
You judge me because I'm not like you
Who are you to judge, maybe I don't want to be like you,
maybe I don't want to be anything that you are and that's
what makes me better
That's what makes me happy

# Lifeguard

I lost everything drowning in life
Swimming through my own problems was the only way to
find myself

# Inner Happiness

Be whoever you want to be
People are going to talk and judge you no matter what
Just remember
You become what you believe makes you happy

## Over Stayed Welcome

It was at that moment I realized I had to let you go as a
friend
No, you're not my enemy
I don't hate you; I just can't push myself to care like I
used too
Your more like an acquaintance
I still want to watch you grow and see all your dreams
come true
Just not in my life not in my circle

# Growth

Anyone can say that they want to see you grow and
prosper
However, stop and notice
Reflect if you may
It's that moment they take action that makes all the
difference

# Today and Tomorrow

Just because two people have had the same person, does not mean you've had the same person

# Breath Taking

I am bold I am original
I'm everything you are not
You ask why
Because I am me and believe it or not
I love who I am

Stop trying to make me something I am not
Or make me something you've always wanted me to be
When you try and change me you'll realize you cant

I love me for me
If you can't love me for who I am
Then you don't deserve me

## Pillow Zzz....

Trying to live the dream
OR maybe I'm just trying to survive the nightmare I've
become complacent too

# Black Mirror

The last few days have been very dark for me
I stare blankly at my reflection to the point I didn't
recognize my own self in the mirror

## Determination

Sometimes life knocks you down and that's ok
No matter what
Life goes on
So giving up is not okay

# Magick

Abracadabra and hocus pocus
Use all the magick you know but remember
You still can't hold me down
I will no longer be a prisoner to you

## Everyday

A walk near a running creek or a jog was a soothing
break for my busy soul
A blessing to escape
Don't run from your problems
Go at them
Embrace them

# Silent Tears

The tears that shed from our eyes
Are nothing compared to the ones that come silently from
our heart
Those are the worst

# My Story

I'm just a man trying to be a hero in his own story

# I'm Not You

You think you're better
Because of your looks and trendy clothes
Nope, you're not
I'm better because I'm beautiful
Just the way I am
I don't need clothes to make me better
I might not be the most popular
However I'll take my real friends
Over fake smiles

## Masterpiece

My writing is my exhale from the world
I feel much better now
Sometimes poetry is just a feeling or emotion needing to
be expressed
It doesn't always rhyme or doesn't always flow perfectly
More similar to a piece of abstract art
Welcome to my showcase of artwork

# Chapter 4
# Unbearable Love

# Me Baby

Some people love being called baby, honey, sugar and
all those sweet nicknames
But I can't lie, I love when your head tilts and you give me
the sweetest smile
Then your lips say my name
That's my favorite

# Lust

You kiss in ways that even my fantasies couldn't imagine

## The Prey

I watched you sip your martini
Lips looking so luscious
Enticing mmmm…
Arousing mmmm….
Oh my,
How I …crave
I yearn…
I…
Hello my name is…

## Belle

Loving you is a masterpiece
Let's embrace a starry night together

## Sexy Perfume

I leaned over to you and said
I like the smell of your perfume
You smiled with a cute giggle then you respond with
Thank you I like your taste

# Penetration

I find myself fluttered and lost
Under every word that you say
Controlling me with the flick of your tongue
Killing me with anticipation
Making me crave you
Enticing my thoughts and body
Breathing heavy for you
Analyzing your every move
Bracing myself to attract
You are mine

# Wishes

I used to look out the window and wish upon shooting
stars
Then one day I opened my eyes and my wish came true
I had you

## Sipping Happiness

All I want is a glass of wine
The only thing I want to wear is a smile
Want to join?

# Midnight Escape

If I undress you with my eyes
And make love to you in my dreams
Can you imagine what I can do in real life?

## Mine oh Mine

My happiness to my heartache
You are my weakness to my strength
You represent my tears of sadness
While still being my tears of joy
You cause weakness in my knees
However
You're the backbone to my determination
Oh, how you are my everything and
I love you for it

# Drowning in Love

It scares me to love you
But
I'd rather live in fear
Than live without you

# Keys to my Country Heart

A cute smile and a bottle of whiskey
Short shorts and cowgirl boots
Pigtails and come get me grin

# On my Lips

I licked your body
Mmmm…
I craved your taste
On my lips
When I lick them
I taste you…

## Love Building

Loving you is like becoming a bodybuilder
It doesn't happen overnight
You must work hard at it
Be dedicated and
Love it with all your heart

# Last call

Whispers in the ear
Kiss me like it's the last time
Have your way with my everything
Fuck me like I'm your dirty secret
One night
Last chance
I'm yours

# Life's Intent

When I think of your love
I smile from within my heart
When I think of being with you
I wish we were never apart

Your love is my compassion
When days are long and cold
Your love is my destiny
When our lives grow old

To be your love forever
Is my life's intent
Your love is my endeavor
For you are heaven sent

# Enlightened Dreams

I dreamed about meeting you everyday
Wished I would have met you in my past
Now I get so excited to know I have you for the rest of my
life
That's why it excites me to say
I love you
Goodnight
See you in the future

# Perfectly

I'm just amazed at how our sharp jagged pieces fit so
perfectly together
I just want to say
I'm lucky to have you in my life
I don't know what the future holds but I can't wait to find
out!

# Long Weekend

Two long nights of happiness
The moments we long together
Sweet memories alongside our love
Now hold this moment of ecstasy
Like it's your last breath…

# Good Morning my Beautiful

Messy hair, chapped lips, and coffee stained teeth seem
to be my new trend
Yet you call me beautiful

Now to brush my hair, apply lip balm and whiten teeth on
my to do list

Because I'll be your beautiful

# Christmas Gift

Beautiful lights across the city
Snow topped houses
Brrr
Cold and breezy
Red noses and sneezy
And a little chilly
Let me warm you up
With some hot chocolate and soft kisses
I love this time of year
More excuses to hold you near
Sitting in front of a burning fireplace
Now let's relax and enjoy our Christmas
Untangle your day
In my arms
Unwrap your robe
Give you the gift you've been waiting for
Show you my love
And all I know

# Warm Smiles

20 years later and you still make me nervous!
Working up the courage just to tell you hi, and your smile
has me lost for words

# First Kiss

That moment you receive a kiss from that special person for the first time
It's the moment in life you feel like you can actually stop time

It starts with the awkward stare, a stare so deep you feel like they undress your soul
Then it's the knots and butterflies start to prevail, followed by the moment you're so close you can feel their breath fall off their lips.
Searching for your lips to shutter them from the loneliness

# Anniversary

I love this day so much
Especially when I sit back and reminisce
On our memories and our first kiss
Laughing and giggling, so bliss

As they say
You stood by my side through my worst
Then without further ado you deserve me at my best
Words can't explain how much I love you so

I thank God for you everyday
For showing me the way
To your love and affection
Making me your selection
Bless it be
An endless love of happiness
Just you and me

# A Toast

To the love we have
The love we could never have
The love we will always have

# Spanish Poetry

## Pesadilla

Odio decir adios
No quiero perder un momento de esos hermosos ojos y
preciosa sonrisa
La unica pesadilla que tengo es no soñarte
Hasta el momento en que abro los ojos y me reuno mi
corazon esta completo

# Amor Antojado

Eres el azucar a mi cafe
Yo quiero ser el chile en tu mango
Tu eres coqueta y picosa
Carinosa y linda

Tu eres mas que belleza
Quitate esa ropa poco a poco
Y ensename el amor que se me antoja

# Fruta Prohibida

Tu eres todo lo que quiero
Todo lo que necesitio
Se me antoja tu fruta
Como el pecado que eres
Porque tu eres my fruta prohibida
Eres la mujer de mi mejor amiga

# Nadie Sabe

Gente me pregunta que es lo que te pasa?
Siempre te ves triste
Pero lo que no saben es que cuando estamos solos
Tu lado salvaje sale

RAWR

Made in the USA
Coppell, TX
04 June 2022

78480942R00089